PRAISE FOR THE
THE UN~~IVERSE~~

"*The Heartbeat of the Universe* gathers poems into a story of the world, past, present, and future, as seen through sound and rhythm, wonder and science. It is a collection that spins and weaves—using both experimental and formal structure—a core connectivity: that we are all, each of us, in every moment, speculative and liminal, and the poetry that recognizes this is truly special. My heartfelt congratulations to the authors and editors of this magnificent book."

—Fran Wilde, Nebula-winning author and occasional battle-poet

"When I first started reading science fiction as a teenager, I always loved discovering the occasional poem tucked in among the short stories and novelettes in the Year's Best collections, and I was so happy when *Analog* and *Asimov's Science Fiction Magazine* carried on the tradition of including poetry in their definition of what science fiction could be. And now this! It's a true delight to see so many wonderful poems in one place! And such an infinite variety! There are poems here exploring virtually everything you can think of:—aliens, ants, quantum entanglement, grocery stores, 1950s sci-fi movies, math, music, Marie Curie, the National History Museum, messages from (and to) the dead, and poetry itself—and ranging from the elegiac to the soaring, the nostalgic to the futuristic, the harsh to the contemplative. A truly galactic collection of science fiction's best poems and poets!"

—Connie Willis, SFWA Grand Master and Hugo-winning author

"This collection constitutes an important step in keeping our appreciation of speculative poetry alive and well, with a remarkable sampling of the diverse voices and approaches poets featured in *Analog* and *Asimov's* over the past decade. In an age when so many challenge the role of poetry in science fiction and fantasy, the editors have taken great care to remind us of how much has been achieved, and how more is yet possible. A commendable achievement, and I look forward to returning to this collection in the years ahead."

—Bryan Thao Worra, former SFPA President (2016-2022)

THE HEARTBEAT OF THE UNIVERSE

Poems from *Asimov's Science Fiction* and
Analog Science Fiction and Fact 2012–2022

Emily Hockaday, Editor

Published by Interstellar Flight Press

The Heartbeat of the Universe: Poems from *Asimov's Science Fiction* and *Analog Science Fiction and Fact* 2012–2022

Text Copyright © 2024 by the Contributors
All rights reserved.

Cover Design by Joy Brienza.
Edited by Emily Hockaday.

Published under license from Penny Publications LLC d/b/a/ Dell Magazines

Published by Interstellar Flight Press
Houston, Texas.
www.interstellarflightpress.com

ISBN (eBook): 978-1-953736-35-2
ISBN (Paperback): 978-1-953736-34-5

CONTENTS

Introduction   ix
Emily Hockaday

THE SUM OF BROKEN PARTS

MOSTLY HYDROGEN   3
Jack Martin

SOMEBODY I USED TO LOVE ASKS ME WHO MARIE   4
CURIE IS
Carly Rubin

POSTULATE 2   5
Timons Esaias

SPARKING THE MATTER   6
Tod McCoy

FAY AJZENBERG-SELOVE (1926–2010)   7
Jessy Randall

SOFT COLLISION   8
Scott E. Green & Herb Kauderer

HYPOTHESIS/ASSERTION   9
Daniel D. Villani

ATOMIC NUMBERS   10
D.A. Xiaolin Spires

MARYAM MIRZAKHANI (1977–2017)   13
Jessy Randall

MATHEMATICS   14
John Ciminello

IMPRESSIONS IN TIME

ALMOST CERTAINLY A TIME TRAVELER   17
Jarod K. Anderson

AFTER NATIONAL GEOGRAPHIC   19
Jason Kahler

RECIPE FOR TIME TRAVEL IN CASE WE LOSE EACH   20
OTHER
Kristian Macaron

ARCHAEOLOGISTS UNCOVER BONES, BIFOCALS, A TRICYCLE   21
Steven Withrow

THE APPEAL OF TIME TRAVEL   22
Kimberly Jones

BILLETS-DOUX   23
Brittany Hause

WHAT A TIME TRAVELER NEEDS MOST   24
Jane Yolen

AT THE NATURAL HISTORY MUSEUM   25
Bruce Boston

TIME TRAVELER AT THE GROCERY STORE CIRCA 1992   26
Kristian Macaron

APOCATASTASIS   28
Jennifer Crow

ABYSS INSIDE OUR YOUNG HEARTS   29
Yuliia Vereta

ENTANGLED PARTICLES

QUANTUM ENTANGLEMENT   33
Ken Poyner

IN THEORY   34
Rebecca Siegel

FIELD NOTES   35
Lola Haskins

THREE-BODY   36
Josh Pearce

NEUROLOGIC   37
Robert Frazier

YES, ANTIMATTER IS REAL   38
Holly Lyn Walrath

ALL THE WEIGHT   39
Holly Day

THE ASTRONAUT'S HEART   40
Robert Borski

LEAVING   41
Bruce McAllister

COLLISIONS   42
Kathryn Fritz

QUANTUM ENTANGLEMENT   43
Fred D. White

DISPATCHES

ANSIBLES   47
Ursula Whitcher

TAXI RIDE   48
Ian Goh

SERVICE INTERRUPTED   50
Levi M. Rubeck

PACKING FOR THE AFTERLIFE   51
Mary Soon Lee

MESSAGING THE DEAD   52
Betsy Aoki

ALL SAINTS DAY   53
Lisa Bellamy

THE TSUCHINOKO ALWAYS LIES   54
Megan Branning

FINAL DISPATCH   55
Robert Frazier

SMALL CERTAINTIES   56
Sara Polsky

WHEN WORDS TAKE FLIGHT   57
Bruce Boston

MILES TO GO BEFORE WE REST   59
G. O. Clark

ATTACK OF THE FIFTY-FOOT WOMAN 60
Ron Koertge

MUSIC REMEMBERS   61
Ashok K. Banker

FIRST CONTACT   63
Stuart Greenhouse

THE IMPENDING APOCALYPSE HELPS ME MAINTAIN 64
PERSPECTIVE
Steven Dondlinger

OFF THE MAP

PAST PLUTO   67
Eric Pinder

WOBBLE   69
Richard Schiffman

TERRA INCOGNITA   70
Fred D. White

THE DOGS OF THE SOVIET SPACE PROGRAM   71
Christopher Cokinos

CONTINUUM   72
G. O. Clark

GALILEO FALLING   73
Stuart Greenhouse

FLIGHT   77
Mack Hassler

HOW TO GO TWELFTH   78
Mary Soon Lee

ECOPOIESIS   79
Joe Haldeman

INSIDE VOICE   80
Jackie Sherbow

I GET A CALL FROM MY ESTRANGED FATHER AND   81
LET IT GO TO VOICEMAIL
Aaron Sandberg

YOUR HOMEWORLD IS GONE   82
Leslie J. Anderson

THE THREE LAWS OF POETICS   83
Stewart C. Baker

Contributor Biographies   85
Acknowledgments   95
Interstellar Flight Press   101

INTRODUCTION

EMILY HOCKADAY

I've heard it said that all poetry is speculative. Just as in speculative fiction, poetry lives in a realm where metaphor is literal and imaginative leaps have no limit. Poetry jumps from dream to reality and back again in a moment, with no warning, and it does not deign to explain itself. Poetry is also inherently mixed-genre. The mundane poem has as much capacity for magic as a speculative one. Poems contain layers of meaning, and these are applied with no concern for literary definitions. A poem about an asteroid visiting the Solar System is also a poem about an absent father; a poem about Marie Curie's achievements is also a poem about a failed relationship. A poem about a black hole is a poem about . . . everything. The future and past and present all bleed together in poetry, and that is just one aspect of its liminal nature that engenders my love for the craft.

Putting together this collection of poems, I realized just how mixed genres can be. In these poems, atoms collide, gravity sings, first contact occurs, hearts are examined—medically and emotionally—and time is traveled: we have poems that look at ancient artifacts and imagine far futures. Trying to sort these poems was almost impossible. Each poem contains multitudes. Mathematics, physics, archaeology, ghostly communication, existential questions—in many pieces these are inextricable. In fact, these poems are so spectacular *because* of how braided these themes are.

I sorted and sorted again, combining piles and reshuffling, trying to put together a story for you—the reader. I hope you enjoy the journey. I know I did. Throughout the collection, we move from the largest cosmic events to the smallest particles, inhabiting mathematicians, scientists, and astronauts, traveling through time via fossil and starship and good old-fashioned time travel, and then to the mysteries of the human heart and quantum entanglement. And on we go, receiving messages across time, space, and even death, trying to understand the other, be it an alien being, a fifty-foot woman, or a family member; and then finally doing what we lovers of science fiction do best: exploration. We end by looking out past our Solar System while also considering the objects within it, even our own planet, which still has plenty of mysteries to uncover. And a future that is right in our hands and rich for the imagination.

May all poetry continue to speculate, and may speculative poetry shine a light not only on possible futures but our lives, grounded and mundane and full of magic.

—Emily Hockaday

THE SUM OF BROKEN PARTS

MOSTLY HYDROGEN

Jack Martin

Somewhere between Earth's axis
and the hippocampus, a line draws
swimmers into water. This is
outer space, blue cloth over borders
with music notes in black enameled writing.
This is how memory works. This is how:
a large system of stars, gas, dust,
and dark matter orbits a common center.
Deep in the ice, bodies get stuck
reaching for the anterograde.
Each meadowlark song is a series
of green sparks. Oh, vastness,
I've forgotten how to be where I am.

SOMEBODY I USED TO LOVE ASKS ME WHO MARIE CURIE IS

Carly Rubin

And that, finally, breaks my heart
although so many potentially
heartbreaking things have already
been said, although I hadn't even known
there was heart left in me to be broken,
but here I am. Because even if we somehow
never-mind those elements she pulled up
from the earth and named as tenderly
as she named her own two daughters,
those gold medals that the French National
Bank refused when she tried to hand
them over to be melted down
for the war efforts of an adopted home,
this was a woman who kept her passion
so tightly at her chest that it turned fatal.
I mean it frankly. This is not a metaphor.
Mme. Curie walked frequently with rods
of radium packed close against her heart
in the pockets of her laboratory dresses,
she slept sometimes with it pillowed
right by her head, decaying alkaline
bonded to decaying woman, until
half a lifetime of exposure killed her.
The story is necessary. It feels unfair
that someone doesn't know, like every
precious gram of burning metal's
been reburied and forgotten,
like Curie was just another
lovesick woman, like everything
is hopeless. I don't know how I got here.
I want to say it wasn't real, my misused love,
I want to beg forgiveness from a grave.
I feel like both betrayer and betrayed.

POSTULATE 2

Timons Esaias

A straight line,
she was told,
goes in opposite directions
simultaneously
never stopping.

My life, she thought,
the knowledge
not helping.

SPARKING THE MATTER

Tod McCoy

Peering out from the awning at the drizzle
that started suddenly while in the bookstore
perusing the physics section
with that person you just met at the chemistry shelf
who holds up a palm in the rain
testing the damp
smelling the petrichor
it strikes you
it's only water
you're not made of paper and glue
the fear of getting wet
is drowned by the thrill of getting wet with
someone who also doesn't care that
the oxygen and hydrogen falling around you
is a tinderbox

FAY AJZENBERG-SELOVE (1926–2010)

Jessy Randall

"Inadequate research publications,"
they told me. So much bull.

There was an inadequacy, though.
No women's bathroom in the science building.

"I'll use the men's," I said.
I didn't escape the Nazis

to let a urinal scare me.
They'd already tried to lower my pay.

As if, I said to them. As if
energy levels of atomic nuclei

can be argued with. As if
physics are negotiable.

SOFT COLLISION

Scott E. Green & Herb Kauderer

Before the order to evacuate,
Bogdan heard the report, the warning Klaxon,
that reactor 4 is critical;

he saw the plume of radiation & gas
from an observation window
in reactor 2 where he was eating lunch.

The plume rising from the breach
in reactor 4's roof seemed so innocent
that he imagines another just like it
reverently moving up the shaft
of the elevator as he descends:

quick death waiting for their soft collision.

But he knows that is not how it works;
death can be slow and lingering
like the elevator ride to the ground floor—

a man named Tsutomu Yamaguchi
survived the atomic bombings
of *both* Nagasaki & Hiroshima
and lived another sixty-five years
before the cancer finally got him.

It has been so long since religion
was open in the Ukraine, so long
since prayers were uttered out loud
that Bogdan can hardly remember
what they sound like;

he tries to rekindle the hope of prayer
currying favor with the fates, if not the gods,
"Let me be like Yamaguchi,
let me see my grandchildren born."

HYPOTHESIS/ASSERTION

Daniel D. Villani

It is hypothesized
That somewhere within $10^{10^{28}}$ meters
Of where we live and breathe
Lie all possible forms of the universe.[1]

It is hypothesized
That within these multiverses
Are beings indistinguishable from you and me.

It is hypothesized
That everything that could possibly happen
Between a You and a Me
Has happened somewhere in these multiverses.

I assert
Without fear of refutation
That nowhere in any of these multiverses
Can be found a Me,
Who has encountered a You
And not loved her.

---

[1] "Parallel Universes," Max Tegmark, *Scientific American*, May 2003.

ATOMIC NUMBERS

D.A. Xiaolin Spires

we played candyland
with the periodic table of elements
you slid down to 79 Au
australia? you asked, packing your bags

gold, i respond,
a ring i slid across your finger
precious metal for your circuit boards

then we climbed 73 steps
and you were six again
pointing at monkeys
feeding the penguins
all the carbon life-forms
held in the artificial zoo

next we rolled an eighty-four
hurried down to 88
to the city hospital
and held hands as
radium-223 alpha particles

battled the cancer
snaking around my
great-uncle's prostate
penetrated deep into his frail bones

as the luminous paints in his bedside clock
blinked 2:26

we trekked to cobalt to cobble alloys
for the jet engine that
we took to the farthest square
put on our masks and suits
and breathed the filtered air

oganesson decayed around us
the fringes of our known elements
bulk of protons and neutrons
the costco of particles
mass clump like a brain
formidable CXVIII

as we returned
we thought about our lives
the Ag in our cupboards

147
plates and bowls
forks and spoons
dishes and suppers
from the accumulation of years

as we glide by iodine
the photographic film reveals
our 53 myriad poses, your victory sign
as you ruffle my hair
my arm clasped around your waist

to atomic number 10
when we first met
you were biting on a cigarette
searching for matches
in front of a dump of a club

i offered you a light

then you released from your lips
a ringed puff, dissipated
wisped up towards
the glow of the red sign
neon

with the letter R blinking
so sometimes twisted script read
COSMIC HEA T
and sometimes it read
COSMIC HEART

D.A. XIAOLIN SPIRES

the luminous rouge of the sign
flickering
reflected in your eyes
in your ruddy cheeks

it was cold

i shivered looking into the sky
thinking how could something so prevalent in the universe
be so rare on earth
a noble gas
your noble chin

MARYAM MIRZAKHANI (1977–2017)

Jessy Randall

I paint mathematics in creatures,
write my notes in Persian. They say
"This article may be too technical
for most readers to understand."
I say try. They say one and I say
infinity. They say dead and I stay dead.
They say study, experiment, postulate,
and I look out the window and see it complete.
They say first. I say, not last.

MATHEMATICS

John Ciminello

I once understood the formulas,
the mathematics of timing,
the algorithms of risk,
the calculus of forgiveness.
Now I'm not so sure.

In my youth I questioned
the square root of sacrifice,
the bleeding radical abundance
nailed to the tree of algebraic marvels.
Now I wonder if I can spare some change.

Then, we relied on the multiplier:
a token of kindness seven times
the reciprocal of grief circulating like
a lucky coin, the currency of children.
Now my pockets are empty.

If I open a book from my youth
and discover a page of arithmetic homework,
would I recognize the penmanship—
the confidence of the sevens,
the passion of the nines,
or the prime mystery of eleven?

Now and then I seek proof in the missing
pieces of this equation,
something less than the sum of all
its broken parts.

Across this gap of time,
this spectrum of differentials,
this range of all things being equal,
I find myself on one side,
and you on the other.

IMPRESSIONS IN TIME

ALMOST CERTAINLY A TIME TRAVELER

Jarod K. Anderson

I think my bones remember, even if I don't.
My teeth feel like time traveler's teeth.
Temporality skitters along my femur
Like centipedes on a fallen branch.

I know how to do it.
When I concentrate on the idea,
Schematics bloom inside my skull,
Vivid diagrams pulsing with déjà vu.

It would take all I own and more,
An absolute and final turning away
From the people I love. From simple comforts.
A gamble aimed at erasing its own necessity.

I'm no daredevil with causality. No crusader.
Erasing the old atrocities would kill our present
And cowardly and selfish as I am
I wouldn't do it for lottery winnings.

I know I wouldn't because I haven't.

But I can imagine reasons
And I ache with the feeling that my life,
As familiar and yielding as an old paperback,
Means that the mission was accomplished.

I am desperately thankful for my own fingers
As if I gave reality a fat lip just to keep them
And each word my wife speaks, love or shopping lists,
Is worth innovation bordering on absurdity.

I can almost remember doing it.

On evenings after work, I take inventory of my life.
I do it for the version of me that made the leap

And if I was bold and brilliant and risked all,

Then, as I watch sitcom reruns in bed,
Safe and whole with my wife softly snoring,
I know I have been well rewarded for my efforts.
I owe it to myself to notice.

AFTER NATIONAL GEOGRAPHIC

Jason Kahler

You say the birds are dinosaurs
and if we visit Antarctica before the snow,
before the tumbling sheets of ice like sharp rag dolls
hand-wave into the ocean,
we'd make way for dromaeosaurs
leaping after protoducks.
More feathers than scales, your dinosaurs.
As a boy I molded from Play-Doh triceratops
who grazed patiently through the backyard grass
I'd ripped free and glued into place
for my shoebox diorama.
If you live long enough the dinosaurs you know
change names. Change shape,
sprout feathers, feel their teeth recede into beaks.
For all they lose—their bluster, their roar—
now the dinosaurs learn to fly.

RECIPE FOR TIME TRAVEL
IN CASE WE LOSE EACH OTHER

Kristian Macaron

snow or a snow globe
Mars at the end of September
that wish I gave you
a map with both our footprints
if you can find one, a wave in a mountain
or a portal under the sea
cherry empanadas or red chile at Christmas
the way it feels to be still
Halloween without candy or candles
a subspace highway without guardrails
or an unbound timepiece
your captured quest or my buried treasure
that bar that was falling apart around us
somewhere in the future
it's not the end of the world yet

ARCHAEOLOGISTS UNCOVER BONES, BIFOCALS, A TRICYCLE

Steven Withrow

once the brave spelunkers hit bottom
not even the light
of history attended them

and the solar torches brought down
would not ignite
in the primordial dark

they were limited to touch
and scrabbled
along the cavern walls

in outmoded postures
like bears
or shamed penitents

of course their voices
were
nothing so old

and one whispered
something's here

in her grip
what once

was a
child's

toy

THE APPEAL OF TIME TRAVEL

Kimberly Jones

Think of the chance to do things over,
to right wrongs, to make the leap,
to relive the past, the thrill,

to remake the time you could have said yes,
the hand you didn't touch, the smile you didn't give,
the kiss that should have lingered, but was cut short
by the need to wash the dishes, or feed the dog
or change the diaper.

Escape back to the time that the beat, beat of the heart
stopped but now could start again
like an engine turning over after it stalled.

Walk through a door; be splintered,
deconstructed molecule by molecule
and refashioned whole, into a new person.

What is the appeal of time travel?
To step through that portal and to
deconstruct and reshape regret
until it is transformed
like sand by a glassblower into
translucent, shimmering orbs ablaze.

BILLETS-DOUX

with a nod to Tom Brinck

Brittany Hause

in brittle limestone
alongside Archaeopteryx
your sneaker print

on a cavern wall
in red and yellow ocher
your waving hands

in crumbling cuneiform
a hasty message
about your day

on rolled papyrus
WISH YOU WERE HERE
in careful hieroglyphs

in colored strands
of knotted llama wool
your ETA

the kettle cooling
as I wait to hear you knock
any minute now

WHAT A TIME TRAVELER NEEDS MOST

Jane Yolen

What a time traveler needs most
when going back to childhood:
a solid plan that can be forgot,
an adventurous spirit that can be curbed,
lust for the road that can turn off to rest,
desire for the next hill that can stop for a drink.
And for the lost times, the loose times, the left times,
the botherations, hesitations, frustrations, privations,
and all the other aberrations
that lead to growing up again:
one good, old-fashioned compass rose.

AT THE NATURAL HISTORY MUSEUM

Bruce Boston

Pinned upon a board
as if they are in midflight,

or still for a second
alighting on a broad leaf,

creatures born for flight,
trapped in a glass case

until they are discarded,
consigned to the dark

of some storage basement.
for newer more exotic

and colorful specimens.
Only those now extinct

remain upon display,
valued for their rarity,

their colors dimming
through the years,

a final statement
to their transience.

TIME TRAVELER AT THE GROCERY STORE CIRCA 1992

Kristian Macaron

Some days it's hard to believe that
there's not something wrong with the
lettuce. It's too green for the world of
dust that's coming. The berries are
machine eyes, but too fragile. You can't
even look at the cherries any more.

Some days it's hard not to think that this
milk has already spoiled in the future.
Not to mention the avocados, so fleeting
they may as well not even exist. You press
fingers into the bread loaf. It reminds you
of a body, already gone.

Some days it's hard to remember what
sleep feels like or quiet, and how blood
is supposed to run through your veins
in a way that is not murmured chaos, or
time rearranging. This version of you was
forged so far from here.

Some days it's hard to not fill a basket with
canned goods or cereals, Fruit Loops, even,
and tell the mother next to you that it's
impossible to buy too much dry pasta, but
that there's something wrong with the lettuce,
probably, and to buy mangoes, while we have them.

It's hard not to notice—some days—that some
of the aisles are already covered in dust, or spend
all the money on first aid. You almost always do.
You walk past the dusted shelves. Something is
wrong with time there. There is such a thing as time travel,
and maybe there is a portal in the aisle next to the freezer.

Some days it's hard to wait by the cash register and
unfill the basket one thing at a time. It feels like
hundreds of things. Your body trembles every time
the bell on the door rings and swings in strangers.
The two halves of you are hope and worry. Some days
it's not the loss, it's the waiting.

APOCATASTASIS

Jennifer Crow

Given time enough, that egg will unbreak itself.
Everything, Plato says, wants to go back
to the perfect state in which it began, so perhaps
Atlantis even now prepares to rise, and maybe
gods will return to their holy mountains,
and your silent pillar of salt
merely waits for the universe to nod permission,
so you can unfold yourself into warm and breathing flesh.

Galaxies unwind, holes fill themselves—
holes fill themselves with dark matter, with meaning,
with the cries of the forgotten—
and stars wink, coquettish spin
turning to dust, congealing, until
reborn, they stretch wide arms made of fire
and embrace your pillar of salt
and make a fire, and blaze.

ABYSS INSIDE OUR YOUNG HEARTS

Yuliia Vereta

Embracing the bottle that my bestie
bought for prolonged depressions,
we are breaking the dawn into pieces,
armed only with smoldering cigarettes
and a couple of hundred strobe lights.
My lungs burst with the laughter,
it turns into engines in shopping carts.
This will never end. This will never stop.
If you once get bored with your gentle life,
we will book you a seat by our side.
There is enough night for everyone.
White Australian dry is just 20 per bottle.
Port wine is even cheaper than that.
There is more hubris in here than space.
It could be enough for the whole country
if it ate nothing but chicken and beans.
The sun rose in the east. It set in my backyard.
We will be young until the end of time.
They will whisper our names and recall *us*,
first-born artificial clones, embryo splits.
We will cross the final frontier and gaze,
hoping to be stared back at.

ENTANGLED PARTICLES

QUANTUM ENTANGLEMENT

Ken Poyner

We look out of the portal
Looking at ourselves looking
At us through a portal.
Each of us raises a hand,
Watching our duplicates move
The same uneventful hands.
We try to think of actions
That accomplished would be
Pristinely unique. But there is
No end to the physics, and certainly
They are thinking of the same
Actions. Each set of us
Has come to the end of our Universe
Expecting an edge of cosmic brilliance

And found it is the middle.

IN THEORY

Rebecca Siegel

Today started like any other day on earth.
Maybe it did for you too. Spring delayed

again. A shower. Feed the cats. Work. Oh
the meetings. What to wear to the damn

meetings. Brushing the snow from the car
windows. It's April in theory. Stopping for

groceries on the way home. Turkeys in the
pigs' field, ancient and glossy, hunting for

last fall's frozen roots. Then suddenly the
internet is full of magic: photographs of a

black hole, the first: fiery, ignited from
numbers and imagination. If a poem

shows you an ermine in its first lines you
can be sure some chickens will die by

the last. Our days are ruled by rules we
culture in our DNA, what can surprise us

anymore? Every spring, the first red buds on
the apple trees surprise me, a kick in the

belly. The hum of the universe shocks me,
the pull of gravity and the way we keep

floating free.

FIELD NOTES

Lola Haskins

1

Myrmecia sanguinea (Wheeler, 1916)

Thousands, perhaps hundreds of thousands lit on the black-thorn bushes atop Mount Armour. Struggling balls of males formed around each mating pair until one by one the balls collapsed and, as their scurrying contents rose up the sides of my boots, even I, a man of science, was afraid.

*

Myrmicia rubra (Farron-White, 1876)

He saw clouds of ants gyrating in the air above a small beech tree near Stonehenge, their paths and intersects like the red dodder that lays its tiny blossoms over gorse. Then the ants spiraled upward like a tree gone to flame and when his cheeks turned hot enough, he joined the others, dancing around the stones.

2

Ants who enslave other ants eventually become incapable of doing anything but fighting and preening and would, if not for the work of their prisoners, starve. E.O. Wilson says there is no conclusion to be drawn from this.

*

Certain beetles introduce themselves to passing ants by raising their abdomens to be licked—rather like a dog offering his bottom to another dog—and releasing a tranquilizing ooze. Then, since the pheromones they emit remind the potential host of his own, they are ceremoniously transported into that worthy's chambers and for the rest of their lives, fed whenever they tap a passing worker with an antenna and present their mouths. Some of these freeloading beetles even change their quarters in winter. Bert Holldobler, writing in *Scientific American*, remains carefully in the realm of insects.

THREE-BODY

Josh Pearce

the heart is a sputnik
the size of your fist
once caught in the influences
of what body tugged
it at a distance,
once sending
radio-rhythmic pulses
across such speechless
voids
now sent to its graveyard
orbit halfway up,
caught in the throat
not quite out the mouth
of sinking sensation
now only a hazard to other
orbiters that may
collide
with it.

NEUROLOGIC

Robert Frazier

Before lipid-exchanged imaging or DNA tagging or MRIs
Before Galvani or the *De Humani Corporis Fabrica* of 1543

The notion of mind seemed widely unformed
Simpler certainly but no less intriguing

For Aristotle considered the brain a kind
Of cooling mechanism for the blood

But from what I've seen of this world
It's the head that inflames the heart

With love's causality and burning losses
While blood strives for a temperate climate

YES, ANTIMATTER IS REAL

Holly Lyn Walrath

In theory, a particle and
its anti-particle have the same
mass. This is not like the thinness
of your shadow. Nor is it like
love. If they touch—mutual annihilation.
We can only observe so much—
the unsolved equations living
in each other's eyes—
this radioactive decay.

ALL THE WEIGHT

Holly Day

When I was very young, and had first learned about atoms and molecules
I imagined that I could see the empty spaces in solid objects
the great swaths of nothing inside of everything,
the thin currents of electricity that barely held things together.
I imagined that I could put my hands through the wall
or my foot through a table, or fall into nothing, like a ghost.

Sometimes I can almost feel myself as that child, can almost see
those yawning gaps in the bones of my house,
in the sidewalk stretching off to the bus stop in the morning
in the bus itself as it comes lumbering down the street,
and I wonder if it's only blind faith that keeps me
from exploding into a clutch of disconnected atoms
flitting off into the cold daylight
like tiny moths or motes of sparkling dust.

THE ASTRONAUT'S HEART

Robert Borski

Untugged by gravity, the heart becomes rounder,
floating like a red balloon

in the antechamber of an astronaut's chest,
deformed by as much as 9.4%.

This we now know from ultrasound scans
conducted in space.

Unleashed, set free, now able to assume
whatever shape it wants,

the organ chooses not a square or triangle,
but a sphere,

as if in imitation of the world
lying bluely below, like a parent's watchful eye.

But also pumping less efficiently now,
yet to be explored are how the heart's other duties

may be affected: its ability to process fast food,
to keep rhythm, to convey oxygen.

And where exactly do the cardiomyopathies of love
and *pi* intersect in this new geometry?

Not to fear, however: no matter how detrimental,
once the astronauts return to Earth,

the heart will be crushed back to normal—
deflated, but never bitter.

LEAVING

Bruce McAllister

What is the human heart but a creature
from another planet waiting for the perfect
moment to abduct us, or should I say *take us
away* from a world we're just not that happy with.

COLLISIONS

Kathryn Fritz

Two neutron stars collided
a hundred and thirty million years ago.
The resulting kilonova rippled out
gravitational eddies and light waves
that reached our blue shores today.
Now, I can prove the incandescent light bouncing off you,
carrying word of the color of your jacket and
the width of your smile,
travels at the same speed as the gravity waves
I would produce
(if I had sufficient mass to affect the curvature of space)
when I trip, falling heels over heart in an arc,
spilling my tea like that kilonova
spewed Earth-sized chunks of gold into the void.

There are smaller crashes.
That man in the cargo shorts
is spooning sugar the density
of Mount Everest into coffee
the mass of a small city
and decades will pass
before we feel the aftershock.

QUANTUM ENTANGLEMENT

Fred D. White

In the quantum cosmos, particles entangle
regardless of their distances apart;

it could well be that both particles
are actually the same particle,

variations of one another,
self as other; other as self,

in two places at the same time—
maybe in an infinity of places at the same time—

which brings me to the matter
of procreation, or rather, the matter-energy

of procreation, whereby $B1 + B2 = E$,
where the lover ($B1$) in rapturous embrace

with the beloved ($B2$), yields energy (E)
of such stupendous force,

that the spacetime tapestry splits open
and again we are born.

DISPATCHES

ANSIBLES

For Adriana.

Ursula Whitcher

I can't explain gravity without using gravity:
the marble rolling round and round,
ridges in stretched rubber,
fabric taut, spiral current
tugging.

I can't explain your message
without piercing or puncture. A syringe
strikes between stars. A fish leaps down
from airless bright.

Your letter cuts between time.
You can't buy toothpaste or toilet paper,
in the stores now, let alone diapers.
Pack a suitcase full, if you come—
you insert a sun here, half-smiling.
You've given the back balcony over to mint.
We hear stray pops, like firecrackers.
Mint leaves curl, wave-edged,
in your yellow sun.

By the time you receive this, I write,
it will be winter. The ice lifts up in sheets.
The tides make cliffs like skyscrapers, falling
up to the green planet.
By the time you receive this light
from my sun, your child will be grown,
an engineer, soldier, a mother,
a fishhook for stars.

TAXI RIDE

Ian Goh

She sits, faint, in the back seat of the cab,
her hair long and dark in the mirrored glass
but gleaming as though she'd just

stepped out of the shower. "Where to?"
I ask, but she doesn't turn to answer.
"Minamihama," she finally whispers,

and we wade through streets of flood water,
an overturned teahouse and the soaked
remains of high schools and hair salons.

When the first waves came and carried
our lives away, others were stolen
from bedrolls as returned bounties

to the sea. Do I tell her her home is no
longer there? Do I mention the dim figures
reposed in puddles by the roadside,

their legs criss-crossed, staring
at starry-eyed glances in the low tide;
of the beast-men prowling the thrice-washed

rice paddies or the firemen at Tagajō
honoring last cries for help—calls that only ceased
once their heads dipped low in prayer

at the head of genkan, long submerged;
of the old ladies and their seat cushions
drenched in afternoon sips of konbu-cha

and last kisses upon foreheads; or the salaryman
who howled in the street to be taken instead.
I do not. Somehow, I know she already knows

these tales. As I turn past a row of lantern-offerings,
I glance into my rearview mirror to see her
staring straight at me. "Have I died?"

she asks, her eyes shimmering like ocean waves
on the eve of a matsuri star festival
before she fades into her doused hearth,

finally home.

SERVICE INTERRUPTED

Levi M. Rubeck

When you say "send me a letter," my pupils cinch up.
The keyboard is backlit with dread. I fixate on food.

Longevity in space depends on the meal schedule.
In between, I develop opinions on trees,

I remain abstinent from entertainment,
I am at the mercy of every dime spent

to put us up here, theoretically divisible
by tenderness.

You send coded messages about the bodies
that swell the cabinet,

they are too fresh for the long night,
lingering with final thoughts.

I write back about our preparations
for palatial visits. Real astronauts know

to pack a picture of what was left behind
but don't ever look at it. Between you and me

the controls are locked, and neither of us
wants to press the talk button first.

PACKING FOR THE AFTERLIFE

Mary Soon Lee

The cadence of her father singing hymns,
sheep baaing to each other,
an Irish accent.

Saturn through a fourteen-inch telescope,
pole-top perched pelicans,
woodsmoke.

Hatteras Beach before the tourists get up,
gull-prints in the sand,
holding hands.

MESSAGING THE DEAD

Betsy Aoki

I watch as the cursor glides across the screen
captured in a chat box, hesitating as in life,
or maybe it's just harder to get the internet
where the dead are. They take turns typing
cryptic messages asking where I am, what
am I wearing, why did I talk more to *her*
instead of *him*. They use acronyms of texting
because each letter travels so far from
echoing minds to my nervous eyeballs.
They always pass the Turing test in triplicate.
When I ask how it is *over there* they evade
comparison: "unspeakable" "indescribable"
"neither hot nor cold, really." The dead
always miss me, but I am just another cursor
in the end, I could be anyone over here,
alive and well, trying to capture their footprints
as they try to capture mine. We cannot touch.
We think we understand. We type and type
worried to find that each has been talking
like the skim of a Ouija board's glide
only to our own twitches and fears
all this time.

ALL SAINTS DAY

Lisa Bellamy

Today they jostle among us until sundown,
listen to our chatter, nudge each other, read the news
over our shoulders; they window-shop,
zoom through revolving doors, sniff new perfumes,
slip into silks, swanky dresses, and at noon on Third Avenue,
walking to Hale and Hearty, I smell my mother's
cigarette smoke. *Hey! You. Not so fast,* I say.
Did you love me? Did I walk into a room and I was
the one person you wanted to see? The old question.
A great cloud of witnesses holds its breath,
waits for her answer—and, as if she were a hurricane
and I a tree, she blows through me: a wordless storm of regret.

THE TSUCHINOKO ALWAYS LIES

Megan Branning

Gravel child, I offer sake now,
so that you might speak.

Fat-bellied serpent, what do you say?
Will you answer, please?

Tell me if the floods will come this year
when the plums are sweet.

Tell me if my sons remember still
how to find this street.

Child of hammer, answer this question.
Will I have long life?

Tell me I will see one hundred years
with my happy wife.

Venom-tooth, will you loosen your tongue?
Words need not be rough.

Tell me raindrops can be filled with pearls.
Tell me I am loved.

FINAL DISPATCH

Robert Frazier

Out where the stars thrum in shortwave
Who'll find this lightship set adrift
Sweep the cosmic dust from my grave
Hoist out my black box treasure trove
Restore the burnt core of my love

No more code to thread and rethread
No new ideas to drive through my head
So discharge my soul in section eight
Convert me to transcendental matter
Lord let me die in an ionized state

SMALL CERTAINTIES

Sara Polsky

The man who answers the phone in customer service
puts me on hold again. He's the fourth one
to swear his system shows nothing wrong
with my on-the-fritz psychic connection,
this high-speed line from me to the future
that predicts morning traffic and each night's chance of rain.
The technology improves all the time, says Rep #4,
back on the line, probably thinking I'm one of those callers
who blames a low-cost ESP hookup for failing to deliver
the big answers, the advance notice of catastrophe
its customers are hoping for. *No*, I say.
All I want is to fix this tiny orange light
that's blinked nonstop since yesterday. I want to know
whether next week is the right time to get tomato plants
and sound quotes for roof repair. I want prediction as advertised:
ordinary clairvoyance and small certainties,
a gentle smoothing of the way.

WHEN WORDS TAKE FLIGHT

Bruce Boston

I experience enchantments
of mythic proportions.
I am the owl and the raven,

the kingfisher, the heron,
the eagle and the hawk.
All birds of prey

forever in flight
or about to take flight,
all birds black in silhouette

against a vellum horizon,
diverse hybrids
of the same inky strain.

I explode to fractal feathers
beneath a semiotic sky
engraved with cloud runes

and clouds glyphs
in a language arcane
and illuminating,

as if words were riven
by endless dichotomies,
an ongoing dialectic,

each thought entrenched
and bastioned by others,
beleaguered by innuendo

and extended hyperbole,
lodged as a riddle
in a complex puzzle box,

BRUCE BOSTON

the aged grain of its wood
darkened and polished
through the centuries

by hands that have
tried to unravel
its wiredrawn intricacy,

by minds that have
tried to unhinge
the sky.

MILES TO GO BEFORE WE REST

G. O. Clark

Behold ultima Thule,
ancient, eyeless, nose-less
and with no mouth to speak of
way out there in the Belt.

A time worn fertility figure,
abandoned after our solar system's
birth and slow formation.

New Horizon's snapshots
taken on the flyby, as if from the
backseat of a speeding car;

time-delayed digital postcards
sent from our solar system's edge,
this side of the heliosphere,

NASA's sophisticated
odometers racking up billions
of more miles, with many yet to
travel before we rest.

ATTACK OF THE FIFTY-FOOT WOMAN

Ron Koertge

After that alien in the desert and the inevitable
radiation, Nancy's life is a spiral staircase

leading up from jealousy and booze and spangly
capri pants to her new career as a giantess.

She'll get around to her husband and that floozy
he's always glued to, but first she tells herself,

Let's enjoy being huge! Look how people reel
when they see her! What a pleasure to step

on that creep who scurries around still trying
to look up her skirt. Heading for Tony's Bar,

she straddles a woman hanging out laundry
who's at first terrified but soon fascinated

as Nancy leans and carefully blows on the clothes,
drying them, making the surprisingly delicate

underthings flutter like white birds.

MUSIC REMEMBERS

Ashok K. Banker

Music remembers
all the memories we forget.
Holds them in safekeeping,
until someday, when stopped at
a red light, a radio in another car
beats an old song and your mouth
floods with cold water.

There is no asking forgiveness
after the light has changed to green
and cars honk and pass you with
fingers raised. Only the memory
of the memories delivered by that
snatch of music and half-
remembered lyrics inserted
between your fingernail and
soft flesh like a splinter.

Why does the mind wander
through breakfast, asking for
bagels when coffee has soured
the taste of greed in boardrooms
filled with hot lawyers wielding
gunmetal laptops. There are no
lyrics to the new song you do not
want to write yet must paint silently
in the emptiness of your apartment
while the half-moon looks
over the dresser and talks
in hieroglyphs of paths
never taken.

There was a day, a monsoon day,
the rain rushed down the hill
and somewhere, a stereo on
Altamont Road played the song

that you danced to while
cars splashed in slow motion.
Spray thundered over the seaface
wall like a sea dragon looming.
You might have kissed once,
perhaps twice,
and her lips were cold
but hot breath on your ear
drew in the notes like a
symphony written on water.

Music remembers all
the details time cannot
hold in its cupped hands,
and saves them in a
monsoon cloud
for future downloads.

Music remembers
what the heart forgets.
And someday, when you least
expect it, and are
stupidly
unprepared,
pays it back,
every last
bad decision,
youthful indiscretion,
wrong turn,
accounted for
with compound
interest.

FIRST CONTACT

Stuart Greenhouse

The alien is new to Earth. The alien has 14 legs. The alien has nowhere to hide, but no one's noticed it anyway. It moves like it belongs. The alien is an Earthling. It's never been anywhere else. It hatched here 45 years ago. It hatched out of the usual 14 eggs, but only 3 of those were alien eggs. The other 3 were earth eggs. The alien mimics your every emotion. The alien is purple and white. The alien is complicated. The alien is disgusting. The alien thinks like an octopus. The alien hides from your fear like a long shadow sidewise a woodcut's intaglio. The alien argues like a shooting star; its anger arriving in its departure, apologetic for neither. The alien sulks when you ignore it. The alien isn't so good at saying goodbye. Hello. English is easier for the alien than Alien. But Alien is easier than silence.

You take the alien to the Grand Canyon. You take the alien to the dog run. You buy the alien a coffee. Stop hurting me, the alien starts saying. No one is hurting the alien, but the alien trusts you, so you say, okay, okay, I'll stop hurting you. I'm ashamed to have tried. Let's talk about something else.

You teach the alien to read. You teach the alien to meditate. You teach the alien what aliens are. Now the alien hates itself. Now the alien is learning.

THE IMPENDING APOCALYPSE HELPS ME MAINTAIN PERSPECTIVE

Steven Dondlinger

The first news commercial advertises luxury
fallout shelters so we are comforted at least
the class system will survive the apocalypse.

The shelters come with water slides and pool tables.
There is a full service bar and a movie theater.
In the back are a bowling alley and a putting green.

They even build them underground
so you can't see your friends
pounding on the windows.

OFF THE MAP

PAST PLUTO

Eric Pinder

Once upon a time
our grandparents chased off the edges
of maps the same swift lions as Sacagawea,
Polo and Vespucci. They gave the beasts
no refuge.

And neither did we. We inherited
an atlas without teeth,
almost complete.

Our ink spilled in neat lines
latticed across hollow continents,
evicting all lions and uncertainty.
Book-binders confined Dr. Livingstone
to footnotes and appendices. His wanderlust
lost allure. We now knew the cubbyholes in which each blade
of grass belonged. The ink dried.
We were never wrong.

Unicorns yielded on every savanna
to the bellows and harrumphs
of ugly, odd-toed ungulates as soon
as surveyors encroached on the blank
spaces of the world. The shady nooks
between mountains blazed
with electricity. The contours
of the ocean floor revealed
themselves to us
like braille.

Even Apollo's chariot obeyed
our terse command to map the dark
side of the moon.

For a generation we knew nothing new
about geography. The wisest waited

for the slow extinction of surprise. Then out beyond
the orbit of Neptune, for one brisk week
the children who had been yawning
with ennui swooned with the messy pleasure
of rediscovery, finding one last land
where there be lions.

WOBBLE

Richard Schiffman

Somewhere, untold light-years away, a star wobbles,
and an astrophysicist on Earth determines that the star
must have a planet, and he estimates how large the planet is,
and how far away it must be from the parent star, and he speculates
that it could have an oxygen-based atmosphere, and a habitable
range of temperatures, conditions in which life might potentially
take root and evolve an intelligent species not unlike our own,
one member of which, at this very moment, may have noticed
the slight wobble of our own Sun, and posited the existence
of our Solar System, and of the Earth, midway in that planetary array,
upon which conditions could be just right to sustain life,
maybe even intelligent life, and while that would certainly be a lot
to conclude based upon the wobble of an unthinkably distant star,
the astrophysicists on both the Earth and that other far off planet
would simultaneously feel a little less alone, knowing that
there might, just might be a member of some advanced race
on another planet on the opposite side of the Universe gazing back
at him (or her) and entertaining at least the theoretical possibility
of their own existence, and thereby, if not exactly validating that
existence, then making it, in an odd way, more palpable to themselves,
which is what love also does—that slightest wobble in a heart
(yours, hers, or maybe both at once) which proves nothing in itself,
but which suggests the possibility that you may have been seen,
or at least deemed likely to exist, by some alien, but intelligent
life-form at the far edge of your corporeal Universe.

TERRA INCOGNITA

Fred D. White

The world is always a map of the world:
think North America circa 1500:
vast empty spaces, terra incognita,
as if some land masses had not formed—
and in a sense, they *had* not: the mind
orchestrates reality, composing
and re-composing the world.
Even computer-precise maps
distort the fractal reality of coastlines,
just as my hands must fail
in their longing to define and redefine
your body, protean as an ocean,
forever (gratefully so!)
beyond my or anyone else's knowing.

THE DOGS OF THE SOVIET SPACE PROGRAM

Christopher Cokinos

In your history of the dogs of the Soviet space program,
you give Laika a splashdown, a wet nose untroubled
by fire boring off the heat shield, that butterfly of plasma
winging down to freedom. She dreams.
A meadow. The one by your trailer with the cats inside,
your mother too, refusing to look at dawn at Comet West.
It hangs there like reentry, like a dog's tail or hero's arm
flung out to the starry utopian collective. Here she is, leaning
so hard against your leg you have to lean back to stay standing.
Was there a secret welcome? How did she find Indiana?
What is home but this distant crackle of sun-warmed gases
making its sound in the crunch of grass and the panting of one dog's breath?
What is going for
if not for coming back?

CONTINUUM

G. O. Clark

Sometimes when you
stop to gaze up at the night sky,
another pauses with you,
the stars a common focal point.

The memory of an old
friend points to the Dippers,
a piece of the puzzle he once learned
on a Scout camping trip.

A ghost arm hugs you tight
around your waste, cold stars above
needle sharp, your last night together
once again nearing its end.

You contemplate what some
writer might have seen, eyes upturned,
all those doorways to other worlds
begging the imagination.

Future astronauts will draw
closer to the stars. Does proximity
breed too much familiarity? Do dreams
become lost in a vacuum?

The night is crowded.
So many ghostly stargazers huddling
together with the living,
the night sky a true continuum.

GALILEO FALLING

In 2003, at the end of its ten-year mission, the Galileo
spacecraft was plunged into Jupiter and destroyed.
Stuart Greenhouse

Just a distant
flyby,

safe as
any other

these ten
years,

then a turn
inward

to the pull
it had

always
banked against

before, then
faster,

falling
only,

a pure
vector,

not long left
now

that the
atmosphere

is nearing,
almost here—

this is no
black hole

event
horizon, but

it might
as well be—

40 gees
of pressure

at its
rarest

topmost
weather

means that
though

no solid
ground

(unless the
hydrogen

at its core
clenched

exotic metallic
beyond our

understanding
might be

in some way
solid-seeming)

waits,
it won't be

needed;
the Galileo

is bending
out of form,

almost
sheet-

metal flat
now—and it

hasn't
even

touched on
the lightest

methane
clouds—

moonlets
in their

last
death-

spirals
don't make it

that much
farther,

why should our
little box

of sight
and thought

think it might
survive

anything
but the outmost

air
this giant is?

We tracked it
in

until it failed
hopeful

to learn something new
but

as our thoughts are
to our own depths,

what it reached
was at best

superficial,
skin-deep,

insubstantial
to the whole.

FLIGHT

for Dennis and Diane

Mack Hassler

"Forty-five miles an hour," Dennis shouted back
As his red and white pure-polished monster
Settled deep and surged due north
Away from L'Anse. We had planned to fish
The Big Lake, but despite marking many at depths
Down several hundred feet, we only caught
The wind and sun.
I thought of Henry Ford, Pequaming,
The loved machines of last century and Neil
Armstrong that boy from Ohio who could fly
Anywhere and, finally, set his polished
Model T of a spacecraft gently down
On the Moon. The sea is full of fish
That can wait another day. We caught the spirit:
Truly blended minds and motors,
Discovery and ancient finds.

HOW TO GO TWELFTH

for Valentina Tereshkova

Mary Soon Lee

Know your place, a woman's place,
eleven paces behind the men
who lead the way.

Know your duty, know how to shine
without ever diminishing
what they did.

Orbit the Earth forty-eight times,
alone, your stomach queasy,
but that view—

that vast untrammeled revelation—
as unequaled, as uneclipsed
as you yourself.

ECOPOIESIS

(NIAC Symposium 2015)

Joe Haldeman

It was a conclave of rocket scientists
sparkling carnival of intellect
earnest descendants of science fiction
looking oddly normal
except for a glow of incipient enthusiasm
kindled by exchange, both
"tell me about your, um, thing" and "let me tell you
something that will change your life"
—and in return he (or she) will open up about
the aragoscope and photonic laser thrusters and SpiderFab
and the 3D photocatalytic air processor
(everybody needs one of those in these polluted days)
but the word that sticks in my mind is

    ecopoiesis

a Whole Earth Catalog word
now twenty-first century—
the quiet song behind everybody's dance
—take some sterile rock of a world
and romance it with science
until it blossoms fecund and alluring
another earth
to try not to
destroy

INSIDE VOICE

Jackie Sherbow

My hands miss the lip
of the ceramic bottle as I try to drink
up all the constellations.
My nephew is nervous at the space
show, and I have to admit
I'm a little scared too.
I want to float
to the top of the planetarium's dome.
I put my hand
on his shoulder and squeeze
it into nothingness, and all the colors
making up the light trip
down my fingers. He
has so many questions I can't answer.
I tell him so many lies.
Later, I'll be surprised
by how vehemently I can believe
that anyone ever needs
to use a quieter voice.

I GET A CALL FROM MY ESTRANGED FATHER AND LET IT GO TO VOICEMAIL

Aaron Sandberg

An asteroid named J002E3
    was spotted
        orbiting Earth,

though not from space,
    it turns out,
        but one of our own—

the third stage of the
    Apollo 12 Saturn V rocket
        sent to circle the sun

found its way back to us,
    some thirty years absent,
        after we jettisoned it out,

hoping to never notice it again,
    now becomes a curious case
        of unstable space junk,

occasionally heading home
    after swinging around
        our star,

whizzing wildly by
    from time to time
        as we squint to chart it

from a cautiously close
    but still safe
        distance.

YOUR HOMEWORLD IS GONE

Leslie J. Anderson

The sand from your childhood
is in the ocean now,
in glass, on the rugs
of a man in Seattle,
a woman in Mumbai.

The carbon you wear
is borrowed.
Your molecules,
the pathways of your mind
shift like dunes.

This sky is not
the one you remember,
and even memory
drifts.

There is no home,
not the home you knew.

There is no you,
not the one you remember.

The ground itself
will give way.
Congratulations,
you are like everything.

THE THREE LAWS OF POETICS

Stewart C. Baker

There is no handbook
showing what a poem needs
but still no poet should
set out to harm, or
through inaction,
cause a poem to be harmed

A poet must obey
the rules of poems
that have come before,
except where these would clash
with Law the First or are,
like the poet's own,
impossible, heartfelt
achings

A poet must protect
their own existence
even if doing so might
harm a poem, even if
this conflicts with
the First or Second Laws
or any other Laws
that they hold dear

As for poetry itself,
that limitless abstraction,
no poet (no matter how
sufficiently advanced)
could ever hope to guess
what "harm" might mean
in the long march of years,
the swoop and swirl of stars,
the ever-changing needs
of humanity

CONTRIBUTOR BIOGRAPHIES

COVER DESIGNER:

Joy Brienza lives in a small shoreline town in Connecticut with her family. The cover designer of the anthology, *Terror of the Crossroads: Tales of Horror, Delusion and the Unknown,* Joy has been at her current job for 11 years as Manager of Design, Websites, and Digital Publishing for *Penny Publications,* publisher of *Dell Magazines* and *Penny Press* books and magazines. Her other creative work also includes designing print, digital, and social media ads, and websites for *Asimov's Science Fiction* and *Analog Science Fiction and Fact* magazines, among many other sites. As an artist, Joy has worked in all types of mediums, but especially loves oil painting. In her free time she enjoys spending time at the beach with family and friends.

EDITOR:

Emily Hockaday is the senior managing editor for *Asimov's Science Fiction Magazine* and *Analog Science Fiction and Fact.* With Jackie Sherbow, she coedited the horror anthology *Terror at the Crossroads.* She is the author of the poetry collections *In a Body* (*Harbor Editions,* 2023) and *Naming the Ghost* (*Cornerstone Press,* 2022), along with six chapbooks. She can be found online at www.emilyhockaday.com.

POETRY CONTRIBUTORS:

Jarod K. Anderson has two best-selling collections of nature poetry, *Field Guide to the Haunted Forest* and *Love Notes from the Hollow Tree,* with a third forthcoming. His literary memoir *Something in the Woods Loves You* (*Timber Press/Hachette,* 2024) explores his lifelong struggle with depression through a lens of love and gratitude for the natural world. Jarod created and voices *The CryptoNaturalist* podcast, a scripted show about real adoration for fictional wildlife. He lives in Ohio between a park and a cemetery. Learn more at jarodkanderson.com.

Leslie J. Anderson lives in a small, white house beside a cemetery with three good dogs and a Roomba. Her poetry and fiction has appeared in *Asimov's,*

Apex, and Strange Horizons, to name a few. Her poetry collection *Take This to Space* is available wherever online books are sold, and her literary horror novel, *The Unmothers,* will be available from *Quirk Books,* August 2024.

Betsy Aoki is a poet, game producer and speculative fiction writer whose writing has been published in *Uncanny Magazine, Strange Horizons, Asimov's Science Fiction, Fireside Magazine, Fantasy Magazine* and *The Deadlands.* Her work was included in the poetic tribute anthology to Ursula K. Le Guin, *Climbing Lightly Through Forests.* Aoki's debut poetry collection about women in technology, *Breakpoint,* was a National Poetry Series Finalist and winner of the Patricia Bibby First Book Award. Its signature poem, "Slouching like a velvet rope," was selected by Pulitzer Prize winner Jericho Brown for the Auburn Witness Poetry Prize.

Stewart C. Baker is an academic librarian and author of speculative fiction, poetry, and interactive fiction. His fiction has appeared in *Nature, Lightspeed,* and *Flash Fiction Online,* among other places, and his poetry has appeared in *Fantasy Magazine, Asimov's,* and numerous haiku magazines. Stewart was born in England, has lived in South Carolina, Japan, and California, and now lives within the traditional homelands of the Luckiamute Band of Kalapuya in western Oregon, along with his family—although if anyone asks, he'll usually say he's from the Internet, where you can find him at infomancy.net.

Ashok Banker is widely acknowledged for pioneering English-language genre fiction in India, English-language television, and series fiction. They have authored over 80 books that have sold over 3 million copies in 32 languages worldwide. Their debut poetry collection represented Young India at the *Salon du Livre* in Paris, 1981. Their poetry has appeared in *Bitterroot, Chandrabhaga, Mundus Artium, Fellowship, Together,* and other literary journals worldwide.As a neurodivergent (AuDHD) and non-binary author of mixed race, low caste and low income background, they are passionate about inclusivity and representation. Originally from Bombay, India, they now live in Southern California.

Lisa Bellamy is the author of *The Northway* (*Terrapin Books*) and *Nectar* (Aurorean Poetry Chapbook Winner). She teaches at The Writers Studio. She has received two Pushcart Prizes, a Fugue Poetry Prize, honorable mention in *The Year's Best Fantasy and Horror,* and has been featured in podcasts, including *The Writer's Almanac.* The U.N. Network on Migration featured her poem "Yoho" in its 2022 exhibition. lisabellamypoet.com

Having a long literary bucket list, **Robert Borski** did not begin to write poetry until well past the age of fifty, but since then has had over four hundred poems published, including two collections *(Blood Wallah, Carpe Noctem).* A former state university system employee, he lives in Stevens Point, Wisconsin.

Bruce Boston is the author of sixty books and chapbooks, including the psychedelic coming-of-age novel *Stained Glass Rain* and the dystopian sf novel *The Guardener's Tale*. His poetry and fiction have appeared in hundreds of publications, most visibly in *Amazing, Analog, Asimov's SF, Daily SF, Weird Tales, Year's Best Fantasy and Horror* (*St. Martin's*) and *Year's Best Horror* (*DAW*), and have received numerous awards, most notably, a Pushcart Prize, the Bram Stoker Award, the *Asimov's* Readers' Award, and the Rhysling and Grand Master Awards of the SFPA. He lives in Ocala, Florida with his wife, writer-artist Marge Simon.

Megan Branning is a youth services librarian in Pittsburgh, where she lives with her husband. She enjoys reading, gaming, and drawing comics. In addition to Asimov's, her writing has been published by *The Magazine of Fantasy & Science Fiction, Space & Time,* and others. Visit her at facebook.com/MeganBranningAuthor.

John Ciminello is the author of three books of prose and poetry: *Shrine Above High Tide* (2011), *Magnolias, Mockingbirds, and Sweet Potato Pies* (2017), and *Bone River Elegy* (2022). His work has appeared in the published anthology *Songs from the Flowering Mountains* (2021). In addition, poems and stories have appeared in *Rain, Analog, Squid Ink, Mentor, Salal Review,* and *The Sun Magazine*.

G. O. Clark's (b. 1945) writing has been published in *Asimov's, Analog, Space & Time, Midnight Under The Big Top, Daily SF, HWA Poetry Showcase VII, Speculatief (BE)* and many other publications over the last 30 plus years. He's the author of 16 poetry collections, the most recent, *Tombstones: Selected Horror Poems,* 2022. His 3rd fiction collection, *Aliens & Others,* came out in 2021. He won the Asimov's Readers Award for poetry in 2001, and was Stoker Award Poetry finalist in 2011. He's retired, and lives in Davis, CA. surrounded by books, music, and enjoying bike rides around town. goclarkpoet.weebly.com

Christopher Cokinos is the author or co-editor of several books, including, most recently, *Still as Bright: An Illuminating History of the Moon from Antiquity to Tomorrow* (*Pegasus Books*) and, with Julie Swarstad Johnson, *Beyond Earth's Edge: The Poetry of Spaceflight* (*UAPress*). He has received awards from the National Science Foundation's Antarctic Visiting Artist and Writer Program and the Rachel Carson Center in Munich. He contributes frequently to the *Los Angeles Times* and *Astronomy* magazine. He lives in Northern Utah with his wife, two cats and several telescopes. christophercokinos.com

Shy and nocturnal, **Jennifer Crow** has rarely been photographed in the wild, but it's rumored that she lives near a waterfall in western New York. Over the past quarter of a century, her work has appeared in a number of genre venues, including *Uncanny Magazine, Asimov's Science Fiction, Analog,* and most recently in the weird western anthology *Along Harrowed Trails.*

Holly Day's poetry has appeared in over 4,000 publications internationally and she is the co-author of the books, *Music Theory for Dummies* and *Music Composition for Dummies.* She currently works as a writing instructor at The Richard Hugo Center in Seattle and at the Loft Literary Center in Minneapolis.

Steven Dondlinger was born in Minneapolis, Minnesota. He began writing in 2012, and his poetry has been featured in *Rattle, Analog,* and the *Canadian Medical Association Journal.* His writing is inspired by long northern winters and a finite existence in an endless universe. He currently practices medicine as a radiologist in the Twin Cities where he lives with his wife and son.

Timons Esaias is a satirist, writer and poet living in Pittsburgh. His works, ranging from literary to genre, have been published in twenty-two languages. He has been a finalist for the British Science Fiction Award, and he won the *Winter Anthology* Contest, the SFPA Poetry Contest, and the Asimov's Readers Award (twice). He was shortlisted for the 2019 Gregory O'Donoghue International Poetry Prize. His full-length Louis-Award-winning collection of poetry—*Why Elephants No Longer Communicate in Greek*—was brought out by *Concrete Wolf.*

My [**Robert Frazier**] father taught cryptography after working with the earliest forerunners of the computer, including Turing's bombes at Bletchley Park during WWII. My mother studied oil painting with Emile Albert Gruppé in Gloucester, MA. Through them the process of deciphering gibberish into plain text somehow meshes with a penchant for impressionistic imagery in both my own landscape painting and in my science-based speculative poetry. The challenge is keeping these influences in balance. And knowing when to free them outside the box in *Asimov's* and *Analog.*

Kathryn Fritz is a poet working out of Kansas City, Missouri. She graduated from Truman State University in 2011 with a B.A. in English, and she currently works as an accounting clerk.

Ian Goh is a writer, educator, and advocate for writing in youth from Singapore. For eight years, he navigated the concrete jungles of teaching English Literature, Philosophy, and Literary Arts. Now, as a Scriptwriter at Ubisoft Singapore, he's swapped chalkboards for keyboards, guiding others in crafting worlds where dragons fly and heroes rise. Who said homework shouldn't involve fighting space pirates?

The late **Scott E. Green** (1951-2016) had a BA in Asian History and an MA in American History. He served four terms as a member of the New Hampshire House of Representatives. In addition to his love of politics, Scott had a love affair with science fiction. This was reflected in his writing '*Contemporary Science Fiction, Fantasy and Horror Poetry: A Resource Guide and Biographical Directory* (*Greenwood Press*, 1989), as well as over 500 poems and three collections. He also served as Vice-President of the National Writers Union, and President of the Science Fiction & Fantasy Poetry Association.

[**Stuart Greenhouse**] lives in New Jersey with his family, writing about memory and chronic illness, often through the lens of science fiction. Author of two chapbooks, *What Remains* (*PSA*, 2005) and *All Architecture* (*End & Shelf Books*, 2007), he has had poems published in journals such as *Boulevard, Paris Review, Ploughshares,* and *Triquarterly*.

Joe Haldeman is the Hugo and Nebula Award-winning author of the science fiction classic novel *The Forever War* as well as twenty other novels. He's been writing poetry all his life and has won the Rhysling Award for his science fiction poetry three times. He's also been chosen a Grand Master by the Science Fiction Writers of America. His latest novel is *Work Done for Hire*.

Lola Haskins' poetry has appeared in *The Atlantic, Georgia Review, Southern Review, London Review of Books, Beloit Poetry Journal, Prairie Schooner, Asimov's Science Fiction* and elsewhere. Her latest collection is *Homelight* (*Charlotte Lit Press*, 2023). Her last, *Asylum* (*University of Pittsburgh*, 2019), was featured in *The New York Times Magazine*. Past honors include the Iowa Poetry Prize, two NEAs, two Florida Book Awards, narrative poetry prizes from *Southern Poetry Review* and *New England Poetry Review*, a Florida's Eden prize for environmental writing, and the Emily Dickinson prize from Poetry Society of America.

Donald M. Hassler, aka Mack Hassler, served as editor of the journal *Extrapolation* from 1989 until 2007. He has published a number of books on literary criticism, including work on Clement, Asimov, Erasmus Darwin, and Arthur Machen. His poetry is much thinner, but he loves to do that also. He retired from the English Department at Kent State in 2014.

Sci-fi and fantasy poetry by **Brittany Hause** has appeared in numerous online venues such as *New Myths* and *Kaleidotrope*. Examples of their work can be found in a smattering of print journals like *Dreams & Nightmares* or *Star*Line,* as well. Brittany's poetry has been nominated for Rhysling and for Dwarf Star awards and can be read in translation to Dutch in the Belgian publication *Speculatief.*

Kimberly Jones has a B.A. in English from San Jose State University and a Masters of Library Science. She is an avid reader of science fiction and fantasy literature and is also an active member of the Romance Writers of America.

Jason Kahler is a teacher, writer, and researcher from Southeast Michigan. His scholarship and creative work have appeared in *Cosmic Horror Monthly*, *Connecticut River Review*, *The Columbia Journal*, *Seneca Review*, *College English*, the *Journal of Contemporary Criminal Justice*, the *Stonecoast Review*, and other publications. His website is jasonkahler.com.

Herb Kauderer is a retired factory worker/truck driver who grew up to become a tenured associate professor of English at Hilbert College. His doctoral dissertation was on Anglo-Canadian SF, and both his master's theses were also related to speculative fiction. He has written film, drama, non-fiction, and short fiction, but is most noted for his poetry. His poem "After" won the *Asimov's* 2016 Readers Award. One of his favorite hobbies is getting physicists drunk so he can understand them.

Ron Koertge is the current poet laureate of South Pasadena, California. His latest book of poems is *I Dreamed I Was Emily Dickinson's Boyfriend* (*Red Hen Press*).

Mary Soon Lee was born and raised in London, but has lived in Pittsburgh for thirty years. She is a Grand Master of the Science Fiction & Fantasy Poetry Association, and three-time winner of both the AnLabReaders' Award and the Rhysling Award. Her latest books are from opposite shores of the poetry ocean: *How to Navigate Our Universe,* containing 128 astronomy poems, and *The Sign of the Dragon,* a novel-length epic fantasy told in poetry. She hides her online presence with a cryptically named website (marysoonlee.com) and an equally cryptic Twitter account (@MarySoonLee).

Kristian Macaron (she/her(s)/ella) resides in Albuquerque, NM. Her full-length poetry collection *Recipe for Time Travel in Case We Lose Each Other* was released from *Game Over Books* in February 2022. Her poetry chapbook, Storm, was released from Swimming with Elephants Publications in 2015. Other prose and poetry publications can be found in *The Normal School Magazine, Uncanny Magazine, Gargoyle Magazine, Asimov's Science Fiction* & others. She works and teaches at the University of New Mexico. View her work at Kristianmacaron.com Instagram: @kmacaron_author

Jack Martin fell in love with science fiction and science fact (the ideas and *Analog,* the magazine) when he was in the 5th grade. He fell in love with poetry about ten years later. Since then, across the years, his poems have appeared in *Agni, Ploughshares, Georgia Review, Fine Madness, Arsenic*

Lobster, and many other journals. He now lives, writes, and looks at the stars from a porch in Ft Collins, Colorado.

Bruce McAllister's short fiction and poetry have appeared over the years in science fiction and fantasy magazines, literary journals, "year's best" volumes, and college readers; and have won or been short-listed for awards from the National Endowment for the Arts, the Nebula, the Hugo, LOCUS, the Shirley Jackson Award, and others. After growing up in Navy family that moved every two years, he's now happily settled near the sea in southern California.

Tod McCoy is a playwright, poet, and fiction writer whose work has appeared in *Asimov's, Felix Futura, Bronies: For the Love of Ponies*, and *Hummingbird Magazine* (forthcoming), among others. His theatre work has been produced in Tempe, Portland, Seattle, and Vancouver, BC. He received an MA in English from Arizona State University, is a graduate and board member of the Clarion West Writers Workshop, and is the publisher behind Hydra House Books, a science fiction and fantasy press. He lives outside of Missoula, Montana, with his artist-witch wife, a goblin child, and a variety of animal familiars.

Josh Pearce has stories and poetry in *Analog, Asimov's, Beneath Ceaseless Skies, Bourbon Penn, Cast of Wonders, Clarkesworld, Diabolical Plots, Interzone, Nature, On Spec, Weird Horror*, and elsewhere. He also reviews films for *Locus Magazine*. Find more of his writing at fictionaljosh.com. One time, Ken Jennings signed his chest.

Eric Pinder is the author of *If All the Animals Came Inside, Counting Dinos, How to Share with a Bear*, and other books about wilderness, wildlife, and weather. He teaches at a small college in the woods of New Hampshire, a few miles down the road less traveled.

Sara Polsky is a writer, editor, and educator in New York City. She is the author of the YA novel *This Is How I Find Her*, and her articles and essays have appeared in *The New Yorker, The Atlantic,* and other publications.

Ken Poyner's collection of short, wiry fiction, *Constant Animals*, and his collections of poetry—*Victims of a Failed Civics* and *The Book of Robot*—can be obtained from Barking Moose Press, at barkingmoosepress.com, or Amazon or Sundial Books at sundialbooks.net. He often serves as strange, bewildering eye-candy at his wife's power lifting affairs. His poetry of late has been sunning in *Analog, Asimov's, Poet Lore, The Kentucky Review;* and his fiction has yowled in *Spank the Carp, Red Truck, Café Irreal, Bellows American Review*. His personal web can be found at kpoyner.com.

Jessy Randall's poems and stories have appeared in *Analog, Asimov's, Nature,* and *Scientific American.* She is the author of *Mathematics for Ladies: Poems on Women in Science* (*Gold SF,* 2022) and *The Path of Most Resistance: More Poems on Women in Science* (*Gold SF,* forthcoming 2025). She is a librarian at Colorado College and her website is bit.ly/JessyRandall.

Levi Rubeck is a poet and critic living in Somerville, MA. His first chapbook of poetry, *Lunar Flare,* was published in 2017 by *Argos Books.* He edits and writes on video games, music, poetry, and more for *Unwinnable* monthly.

Carly Rubin holds an MFA in Creative Writing from the City College of New York and a PhD in English from Louisiana State University. Her writing has appeared on NPR's *RadioLab,* in the *Harvard Review,* in *Meridian's Best New Poets,* and elsewhere. She is currently at work on a book manuscript based on her doctoral dissertation, as well as on a collection of poems. Carly works in strategy and business development for Via Transportation, a transit tech company. She is based in Brooklyn, New York.

Aaron Sandberg has appeared or is forthcoming in *The Offing, Lost Balloon, Flash Frog, Phantom Kangaroo, Qu, No Contact, West Trade Review, Alien Magazine, Whale Road Review,* and elsewhere. Nominated for The Pushcart Prize, Best of the Net, and the Dwarf Stars Award, you can see him—and his writing—on Instagram @aarondsandberg.

Richard Schiffman is an environmental reporter, poet and author of two biographies based in New York City. His poems have appeared on the BBC and on NPR as well as in the *Alaska Quarterly, New Ohio Review, Christian Science Monitor, The New York Times, Writer's Almanac, This American Life in Poetry, Verse Daily* and other publications. His first poetry collection *What the Dust Doesn't Know* was published in 2017 by *Salmon Poetry.*

Jackie Sherbow is a Queens, NYC based publisher, editor, writer, and author of the chapbook *Harbinger* (*Finishing Line Press,* 2019). Jackie's poems have appeared or are in places like *Sierra Nevada Review, Coffin Bell, Luna Luna,* and *Day One.* Their short stories have appeared in *Mystery Magazine* and *The Beat of Black Wings* (*Untreed Reads*). Jackie works as the senior managing editor for *Alfred Hitchcock's Mystery Magazine* and *Ellery Queen's Mystery Magazine* and serves on the board of directors of *Newtown Literary.* They are the founding publisher at *THRASH Press.*

Rebecca Siegel lives and writes in Vermont. A two-time Pushcart Prize nominee, her poems have appeared in *boats against the current, Moist Poetry Journal, Bloodroot Literary Magazine, Pinhole Poetry, Visual Verse, Dust Poetry Magazine, Analog Magazine, Goat's Milk Magazine, Zócalo Public Square, Container's Multitudes* series, *Straight Forward Poetry,* and elsewhere.

D. A. Xiaolin Spires steps into portals and reappears in sites such as Hawai'i, NY, various parts of Asia and elsewhere, with her keyboard appendage attached. Her work appears in publications such as *Clarkesworld, Analog, Nature, Terraform, Fireside, Star*Line, Uncanny* and anthologies such as *Make Shift, Life Beyond Us, Ride the Star Wind, Sharp and Sugar Tooth, Deep Signal,* and *Battling in All Her Finery.* Select stories can be read in German, Spanish, Vietnamese, Estonian, French and Japanese translation. She can be found on Twitter @spireswriter, on Mastodon: wandering.shop/@ spireswriter, on Bluesky spires.bsky.social/ and on her website: daxiaolinspires.wordpress.com.

Yuliia Vereta is a Polish writer of Ukrainian origin, whose speculative works were published in print and online among others in *Star*Line, Asimov's Science Fiction, Leading Edge, Penumbric, Kaleidotrope, Parsec, Aphelion, Dissections, Bewildering Stories* and *Pressfuls Press Anthologies.* She holds an M.A. in translation and currently works as a translator in Katowice.

Dr. Daniel Villani was born in 1947. After learning to read, ca. 1953, he found it difficult to distinguish (a) science fiction from (b) science fact. This led to him choosing a career path dedicated to helping move category (a) items, including Pioneer Venus, Galileo Probe, Magellan Radar Mapper, assorted communication satellites, and Dragon, into category (b). His path to that career passed through Caltech and a 1967 religious conference. His future wife, another conference attendee, was a Beatles fan. He could play the guitar/sitar part in "Norwegian Wood." The rest is biography.

Holly Lyn Walrath is a writer, editor, and publisher. Her poetry and short fiction has appeared in *Strange Horizons, Fireside Fiction, Analog,* and *Flash Fiction Online.* She is the author of several books of poetry, including *Glimmerglass Girl* (2018), and *The Smallest of Bones* (2021), and *Numinose Stones* (2023). She holds a B.A. in English from The University of Texas and a Master's in Creative Writing from the University of Denver. In 2019, she launched Interstellar Flight Press, an indie SFF publisher dedicated to publishing underrepresented genres and voices. Find her online at hlwalrath.com.

Steven Withrow has authored three chapbooks—*The Sun Ships, The Bedlam Philharmonic,* and *The Nothing Box*—and a collaborative collection, *The Exorcised Lyric,* with Frank Coffman. His speculative and dark fantasy poems have appeared in *Asimov's Science Fiction, Spectral Realms, Space & Time,* and *Dreams & Nightmares.* His work was nominated for the Rhysling and Elgin awards, and he wrote the libretto for a chamber opera based on a classic English ghost story. He lives on Cape Cod.

Ursula Whitcher is a mathematician and editor whose household has a one-to-one correspondence between cats and humans. Find links to Ursula's poetry, prose, and social media at yarntheory.net, or look for the collection of linked short stories *North Continent Ribbon* from *Neon Hemlock Press*.

Fred D. White's poetry has appeared in many periodicals in addition to *Asimov's* and *Analog*, including *The American Journal of Poetry*, *Common Ground Review*, and *Rattle*. A professor of English, emeritus (Santa Clara University), his books include *The Writer's Idea Thesaurus*, *The Daily Writer*, *Writing Flash*, and *Approaching Emily Dickinson*. He lives in Folsom, CA.

Jane Yolen's 449th book is about to hit the bookstores (she has fourteen new books this fall and spring). A good number of them are books of poetry. She has won the Asimov'v's Poetry poll a number of times, and she sends out a poem a day to over a thousand subscribers. Her website is janeyolen.com where you can ask questions that she answers once a week. Her three children and two of her five grandchildren are published authors as well.

ACKNOWLEDGMENTS

Grateful acknowledgment is made to the following for permission to reprint their copyrighted material.

"Abyss Inside Our Young Hearts" by Yuliia Vereta, Copyright © 2021 by Yuliia Vereta, reprinted by permission of the author. First appeared in *Asimov's Science Fiction Magazine*.

"After National Geographic" by Jason Kahler, Copyright © 2020 by Jason Kahler, reprinted by permission of the author. First appeared in *Analog Science Fiction and Fact*.

"All Saints Day" by Lisa Bellamy, Copyright © 2015 by Lisa Bellamy, reprinted by permission of the author. First appeared in *Asimov's Science Fiction Magazine*.

"All the Weight" by Holly Day, Copyright © 2018 by Holly Day, reprinted by permission of the author. First appeared in *Asimov's Science Fiction Magazine*.

"Almost Certainly a Time Traveler" by Jarod K. Anderson, Copyright © 2016 by Jarod K. Anderson, reprinted by permission of the author. First appeared in *Asimov's Science Fiction Magazine*.

"Ansibles" by Ursula Whitcher, Copyright © 2020 by Ursula Whitcher, reprinted by permission of the author. First appeared in *Asimov's Science Fiction Magazine*.

"Apocatastasis" by Jennifer Crow, Copyright © 2017 by Jennifer Crow, reprinted by permission of the author. First appeared in *Asimov's Science Fiction Magazine*.

"Archaeologists Uncover Bones, Bifocals, a Tricycle" by Steven Withrow, Copyright © 2019 by Steven Withrow, reprinted by permission of the author. First appeared in *Asimov's Science Fiction Magazine*.

INTERSTELLAR FLIGHT PRESS

Interstellar Flight Press is an indie speculative publishing house. We feature innovative works from the best new writers in science fiction and fantasy. In the words of Ursula K. Le Guin, we need "writers who can see alternatives to how we live now, can see through our fear-stricken society and its obsessive technologies to other ways of being, and even imagine real grounds for hope."

Find us online at www.interstellarflightpress.com.

facebook.com/interstellarflightpress

twitter.com/intflightpress

instagram.com/interstellarflightpress

patreon.com/interstellarflightpress

Printed in the USA
CPSIA information can be obtained
at www.ICGtesting.com
JSHW021909120524
62807JS00001B/66

9 781953 736345